CONTENTS

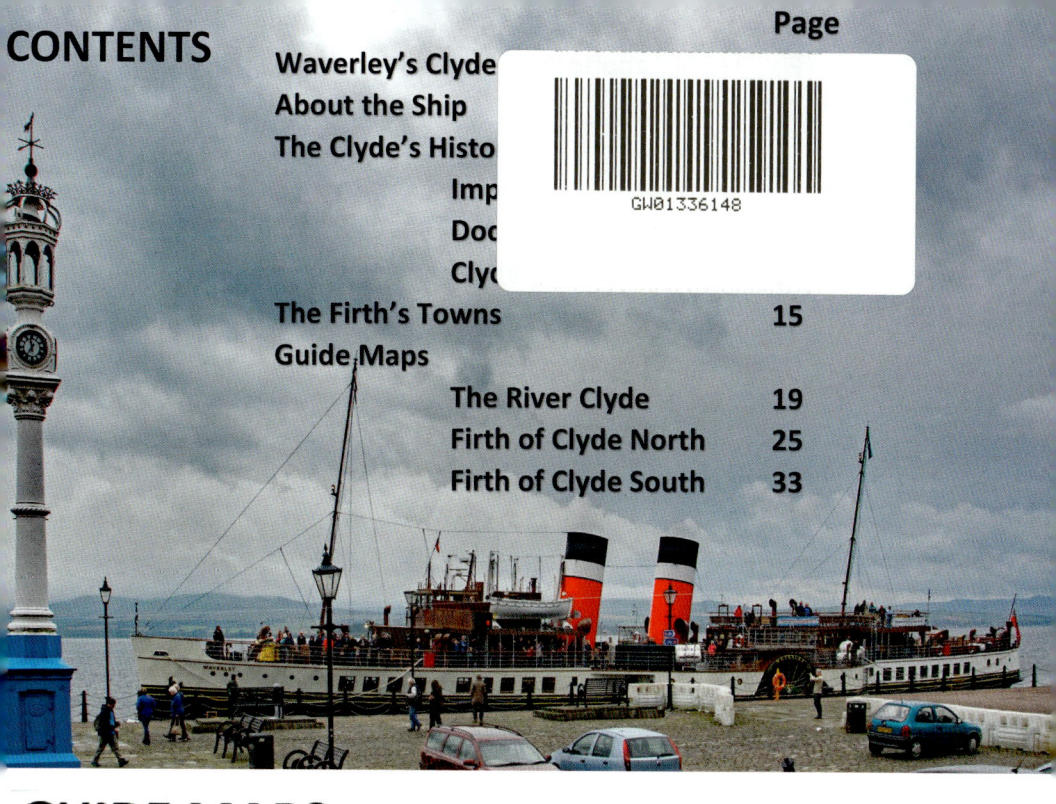

	Page
Waverley's Clyde	
About the Ship	
The Clyde's History	
Imp...	
Doc...	
Cly...	
The Firth's Towns	15
Guide Maps	
The River Clyde	19
Firth of Clyde North	25
Firth of Clyde South	33

GUIDE MAPS

The River Clyde
1. From the city
2. To the sea

Firth of Clyde North
3. The Channel
4. Loch Long
5. Kyles of Bute

Firth of Clyde South
6. Golf Coast
7. Arran & South Bute
8. Kintyre

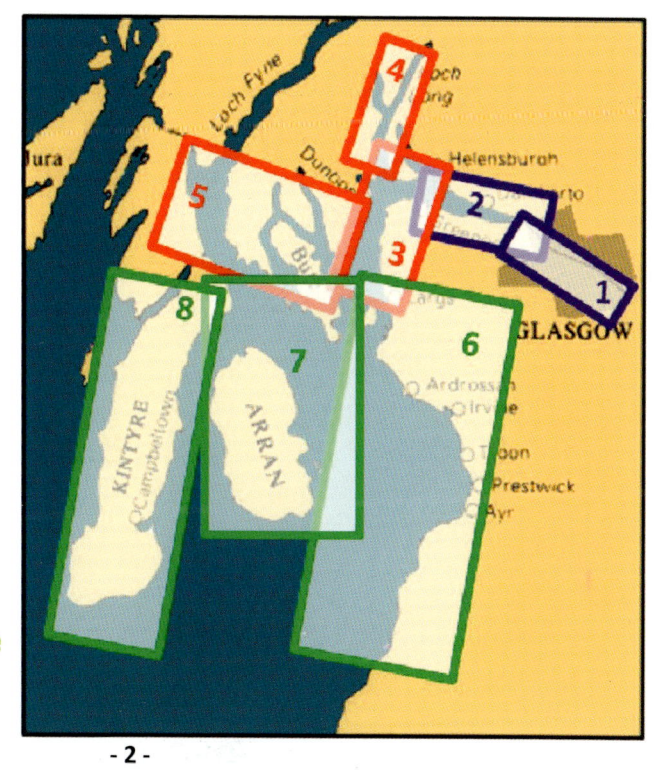

- 2 -

Waverley's Clyde Operations

Running a paddle steamer today is a complex operation. Waverley is quite different to a conventional ship and so it is difficult to apply modern marine legislation to her. Maintaining the ship is also a challenge.

Arrangements for navigation in the Firth of Clyde as far as the Isle of Arran are the responsibility of Clydeport who also act as passenger registrar and so are advised of Waverley's passenger numbers as they are counted on and off the ship at each pier.

North of Little Cumbrae island, ships require a pilot. Clydeport has eight pilots who meet arriving ships. However, Waverley's Captain has a pilotage exemption which requires experience of the area and an appropriate exam to be passed.

Waverley is steered by her rudder which, unlike other ships, has no propeller in front of it. This makes the rudder ineffective at low speed. One advantage of her large paddles, however, is that they enable the ship to stop in her own length.

To maintain her steering Waverley has to approach piers faster than other ships but can then stop quickly. Ropes are then used to position the ship against the pier. This is a specialised operation that requires effective teamwork between the bridge officers, engineers and deckhands.

Clyde Piers

During the heyday of Clyde steamers there were approximately 70 piers, many being the only access for remote communities. Most of these piers were extensively used so it was not difficult to justify expenditure on their construction and maintenance. For example, the quarter mile long pier at Whiting Bay, the longest pier in Scotland, was justified because of its frequent traffic.

Today, with only one paddle steamer on the Clyde, funding pier maintenance can be difficult. However, support from Councils and pier authorities generally enables Waverley to maintain her Clyde timetable although some piers have been lost.

When Waverley entered service in 1947 she was based at Craigendoran pier until its closure in 1972. One of her regular routes was from Craigendoran to Lochgoilhead and Arrochar via Rothesay, Dunoon and Blairmore.

The pier at Lochgoilhead closed in 1965 and the pier at Arrochar closed in 1972. Other notable long-gone piers used by Waverley were Whiting Bay (she was the last steamer to call there when the pier closed 1961), Innellan (closed 1972) and Inveraray (closed 1973) which was a 90-mile steamer trip from Glasgow.

After Waverley was gifted to the PSPS (Scottish Branch) for £1 in 1974, her sailings continued to be affected by changes in available piers. In 1978 Helensburgh pier, which had been closed to steamers in 1952, was dredged to allow Waverley to use it.

Other re-opened piers were Lochranza, rebuilt in 2003 and Blairmore, where Waverley had called on her maiden voyage on 16th June 1947. The establishment of the Friends of Blairmore pier in 2004 led to the pier's re-opening in 2005.

Prior to its re-opening she last called at the pier in 1997 after which its deteriorating condition prevented further calls. There is another active pier association at Tighnabruaich, formed in 1999. Since then it has provided an exhibition in the former Pier master's Office and lobbied Argyll and Bute Council to replace rotten timbers at the pier head.

Dunoon's iconic wooden pier was closed in 2004 when a new linkspan was built. As a result, Waverley now calls at the breakwater. In 2015/16 the old pier received a £3 million makeover, although no berthing facilities were provided.

Waverley's Glasgow departure point was moved downstream from Anderston Quay to Pacific Quay in 2004 due to the construction of the "Squinty Bridge".

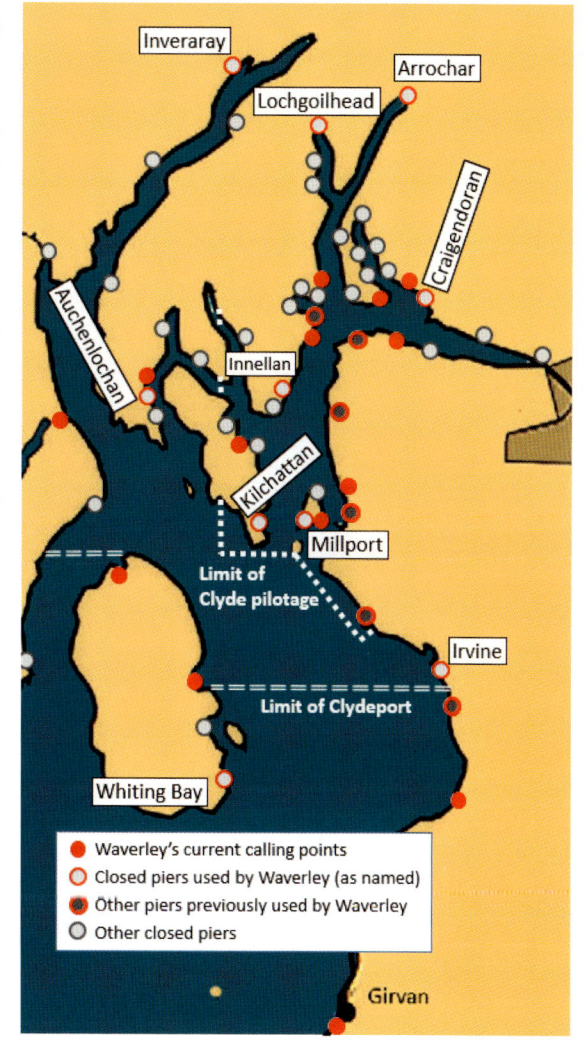

Tarbert pier was repaired in 2011 to ensure that Waverley could continue to call there. In 2008/09 Largs pier was also rebuilt, during which Waverley served Largs from Fairlie pier, two miles to the south of the town.

The pier at Millport was permanently closed following storm damage in January 2014. Fortunately, Waverley continues to call at Great Cumbrae Island as the pier at Keppel was made available to the ship.

Waverley currently has sixteen ports of call on the Clyde. Although maintaining piers can be an expensive business, the ship provides an important contribution to British tourism for which the total economic benefits have been calculated to benefit the British economy by £7.3 million each year.

About the Ship

Waverley was built by A&J Inglis at Pointhouse on Glasgow's River Kelvin, now the site of the Riverside Museum. Her hull is 240 feet long, 58 feet wide and is of a traditional construction with frames and riveted plates. She has a 6 foot draft and has a gross tonnage of 693. Waverley was originally certificated to carry 1350 passengers but now can carry up to 860 on three main decks.

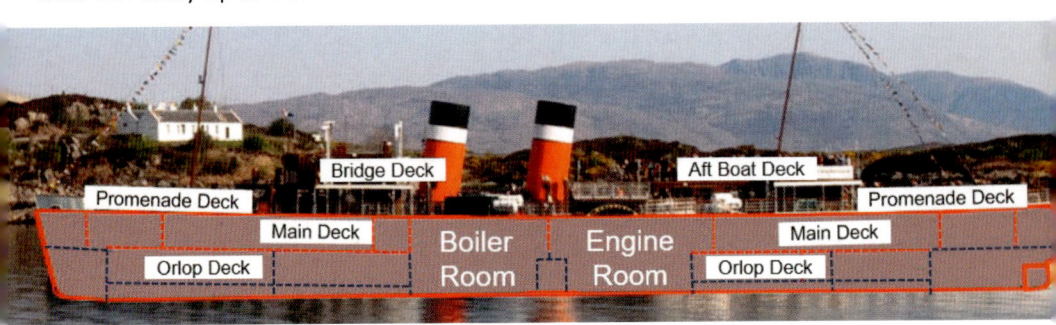

Waverley was built to replace the original PS Waverley, built in 1899, that was sunk off Dunkirk after being attacked by 12 Heinkel bombers and hit by three bombs. She was built for the London & North Eastern Railway Company and transferred to Caledonian Steam Packet Company in 1948 and Caledonian MacBrayne (CalMac) in 1973.

After she was launched she was towed to Greenock where her engines, paddles, boiler and funnels were fitted. The boiler was a double ended Scotch boiler with six furnaces. Due to post-war shortages it was originally coal fired and was converted to oil-firing in 1957. In 1981 the boiler was replaced by a more efficient twin furnace Babcock Steambloc boiler.

Waverley was extensively rebuilt in 2000 and 2003 funded by a £7 million heritage lottery grant. As part of this the 1981 boiler was replaced by two 'Thermax' boilers made by Cochrane of Annan.

Key dates:

- 2.10.46 Launched
- 16.6.47 Maiden voyage
- 2.10.73 Withdrawn from service
- 8.8.74   CalMac sell Waverley to PSPS for £1
- 22.5.75 Maiden voyage in preservation

Waverley has sailed on the Clyde every year since 1975.

Photo: Wikimedia Commons — A&J Inglis Shipyard in 1930

Waverley achieved 18.37 knots during her sea trials off Skelmorlie in 1947

Waverley's engine was built by Rankin and Blackmore in Greenock. It is a 2,100 h.p. diagonal triple expansion engine with cylinders of 24, 39 and 62 inch diameter. The engine normally operates at 44 rpm to give a 13 knot service speed. The ship's maximum speed is 18 knots when the engine operates at 57 rpm.

The main engine is one of 11 steam engines on the ship. When the ship was originally built there were many more as all auxiliaries were steam powered. Now there are diesel generators that power the fans and some of the pumps.

The engine's crankshaft drives the paddle wheels so they cannot rotate independently. These are 17 feet across and each has 8 floats of 11 feet by 3 feet. For maximum efficiency, the floats have a feathering mechanism.

In the past parts of her steam machinery would have been maintained by specialists in the Clyde's shipyards.

During the winter months Waverley's engineering team and volunteers maintain the engine, boilers, paddles, toilets and deck gear whilst the ship is moored at Pacific Quay, Glasgow. The ship is dry-docked in Greenock for two to three weeks, usually in April. This includes a full hull survey, painting and repairs.

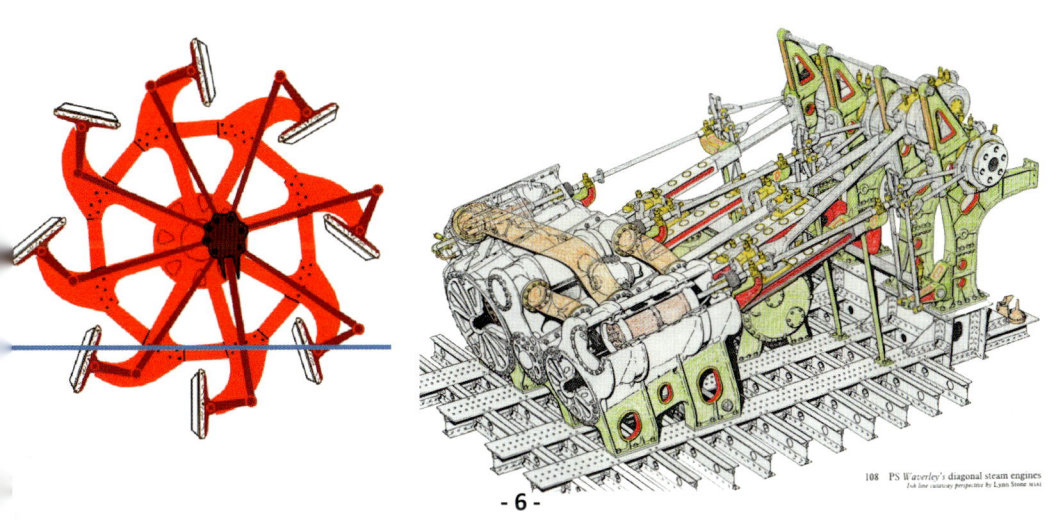

The Clyde's History

At 109 miles long, the River Clyde is Britain's eighth longest river. It rises in the Lowther Hills a few miles from the River Tweed to reach the sea at the Firth of Clyde which has the largest and deepest coastal waters in the British Isles. It has been an important sea route from the earliest times.

The act of union in 1707 increased trade along the Clyde to Glasgow, especially that of tobacco. However the Firth was hazardous and the river to Glasgow was too shallow for sea-going ships.

Improving Navigation

The first navigational light to be provided on the Clyde was an open fire at Little Cumbrae in 1757 which was replaced by a lighthouse in 1793. Another such beacon was established in 1776 at Lady Isle, off Troon. Keeping island beacons supplied and lit in all weathers would have been a challenging task.

The Clyde's first lighthouse was built at Pladda in 1790. This was followed by those at Little Cumbrae (1793), Cloch (1797), Toward Point (1812), Turnberry (1873), Holy Isle inner (1877), Ailsa Craig (1886), Gantocks (1886), Lady Isle (1903) and Holy Isle outer (1905).

Before the Clyde was deepened, seagoing ships could only reach the anchorage by Newark Castle, it was here Glasgow's merchants leased land for a harbour. By 1710 this had the Clyde's principal custom house and became known as 'Port Glasgow'.

With increasing trade something had to be done to get sea-going ships to Glasgow. This was the construction of the Lang Dyke in 1775 which deepened the Clyde channel by both increasing tidal scour to prevent southern sandbanks filling the dredged channel and changing the water flow so that it directly washed away the river bottom.

However considerable dredging to further deepen and widen the channel was required for ships to reach Glasgow. Much of this was done in the 1850s. However this project was not completed until the 1880s due to the time taken to blast away volcanic rock at Renfrew. There is now a 24 ft. deep channel to Glasgow. Prior to the construction of the Lang Dyke it was barely four feet.

No deepening is required for the Finnart Oil terminal in Loch Long. Here the natural channel and steep sided loch provide a natural channel with a minimum depth of 120 ft. from the sea to the terminal's jetty. Hunterston, just south of Largs, also has a deep 130 ft. jetty for its ore and coal carriers. Greenock's Clydeport, which handles container and cruise ships, has a depth of 41 ft.

CLYDE LIGHTS (B)eacon (L)ighthouse

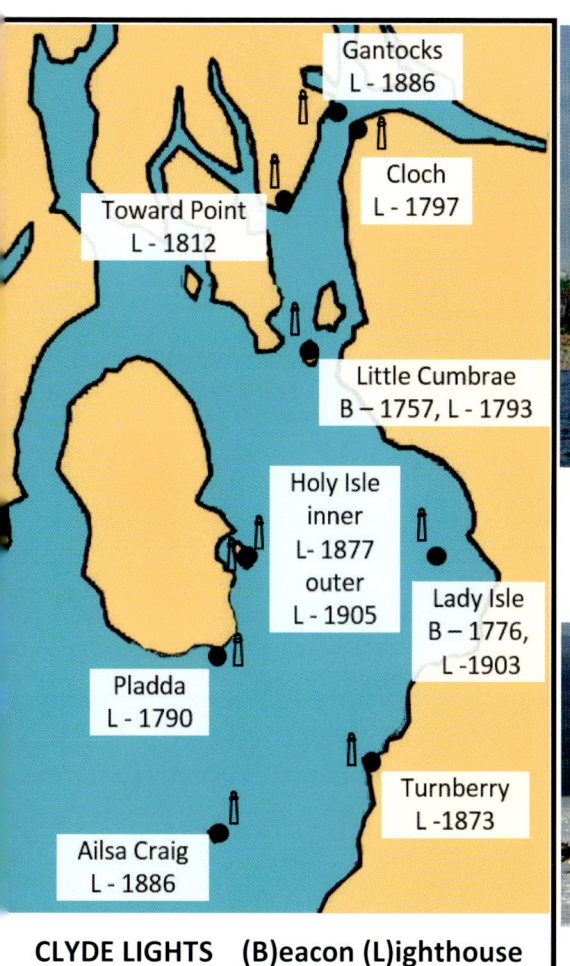

Map labels:
- Gantocks L - 1886
- Cloch L - 1797
- Toward Point L - 1812
- Little Cumbrae B - 1757, L - 1793
- Holy Isle inner L - 1877, outer L - 1905
- Lady Isle B - 1776, L - 1903
- Pladda L - 1790
- Turnberry L - 1873
- Ailsa Craig L - 1886

Pladda lighthouse was built in 1790 before lighthouses had identifying flashes. Hence the separate upper and lower lighthouses identify its location.

Gantocks beacon

The channel formed by the Lang Dyke

Glasgow's Docks

When sea-going ships first reached Glasgow they docked at the Broomielaw quays. In 1823 the length of the quays was 865 yards. By 1860, they were 3860 yards long. The first dock to be constructed was the small Kingston Dock which opened in 1867 and was infilled in 1966 for the construction of the Kingston Bridge.

In 1880 the Queen's Dock at Finnieston was opened. This added nearly two miles of additional wharfs. It was used by ships for South Africa (Clan Line), India (City Line) and North America (Donaldson Line). Prince's Dock, on the other side of the river, was completed in 1897 and provided a further two miles of wharves. Shipping lines using this dock included the Canadian Pacific Company and Anchor-Donaldson Line. West of the River Kelvin, Merklands Lairage opened in 1907 for livestock. Meadowside Quay opened in 1912 and had huge elevators for grain from the American prairies.

Rothesay dock, for coal, opened in 1907. In 1910 Yorkhill dock gave the Anchor Line berths for its New York passenger liners. The King George V Dock was completed in 1931 and is now the only working dock in this stretch of the Clyde. The Clyde was particularly important during WW2 when it was Britain's main assembly and reception point for shipping convoys. It was also an important naval base. There was an anti-submarine boom between the Cloch lighthouse and Dunoon.

At their peak, the city's docks had 10 miles of quayside, with travelling cranes, transit sheds and a complex railway network. With bigger ships and containerisation traffic declined from the 1950s. Queen's and Prince's docks closed in 1970 and were filled in

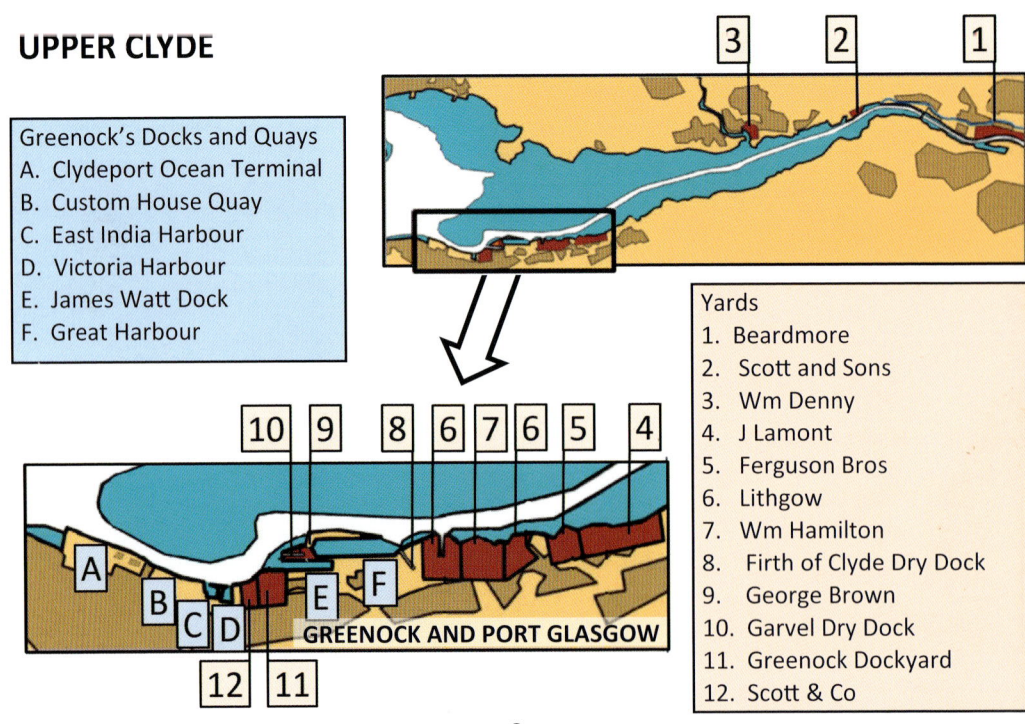

UPPER CLYDE

Greenock's Docks and Quays
A. Clydeport Ocean Terminal
B. Custom House Quay
C. East India Harbour
D. Victoria Harbour
E. James Watt Dock
F. Great Harbour

Yards
1. Beardmore
2. Scott and Sons
3. Wm Denny
4. J Lamont
5. Ferguson Bros
6. Lithgow
7. Wm Hamilton
8. Firth of Clyde Dry Dock
9. George Brown
10. Garvel Dry Dock
11. Greenock Dockyard
12. Scott & Co

GREENOCK AND PORT GLASGOW

using rubble from St Enoch Station and its hotel. Only the Prince's dock canting basin remains.

The Clyde's most modern dock is Greenock's Clydeport Container Terminal (now the Ocean Terminal) opened in 1970 and has a 41 ft deep berth which also takes cruise ships.

Shipbuilding

With a deep channel and easy availability of coal and iron ore, Glasgow became Britain's greatest seaport and shipbuilding centre. Since the founding of Scott's yard in Greenock in 1712, it is estimated that 25,000 ships have been built on the River Clyde and its Firth. Denny of Dumbarton alone built over 1,500 ships between 1844 and 1962. Other famous yards were John Brown, Fairfield, Scott Lithgow and Harland & Wolf.

Just after WW2, Clyde shipyards built around a quarter of the world's merchant shipping fleet. Soon afterwards the shipping industry declined and the only Clyde shipbuilding is now at BAE Systems Govan Yard and Ferguson's in Port Glasgow.

The Finnieston crane is a landmark of both Glasgow's marine heritage and another major industry, railway workshops. Built in 1931, this was primarily used to load large steam locomotives onto ships for export throughout the world. It was last used in the late 1990s for the export of large gas turbines made by John Brown Engineering Ltd.

GLASGOW AND CLYDEBANK

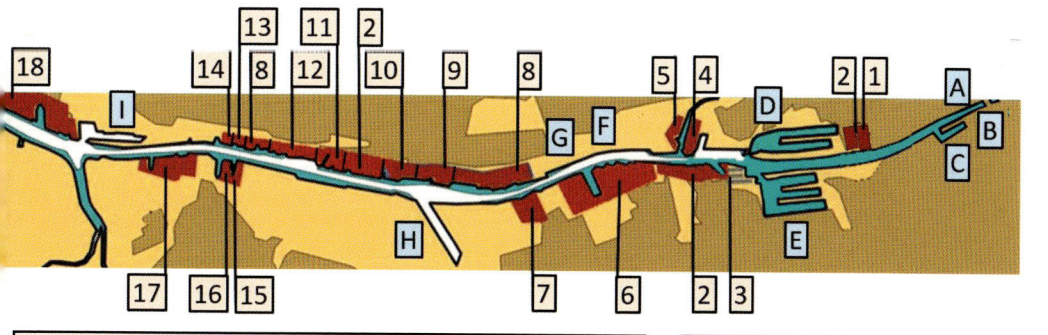

Yards
1. David Rowan
2. Harland & Wolff
3. Govan Graving Docks
4. A&J Inglis
5. D&W Henderson
6. Fairfield
7. Alexander Stephen & Sons
8. Barclay, Curle
9. Charles Connell
10. Mechan's
11. Blythswood
12. Yarrow
13. Drysdale's Pump
14. Bull's Propellers
15. H MacLean
16. Clyde Trust Works
17. Simons-Lobnitz
18. John Brown

Docks and Quays
A Broomielaw
B Bridge Wharf
C Kingston Dock
D Queen's Dock
E Prince's Dock
F Meadowside Quay
G Merklands Quay
H King George V Dock
I Rothesay Dock

All that remains of Queen's and Prince's dock today

| 1. Harbour tunnel rotundas | 2. Canting basin | 3. Waverley's departure point |

Paddle Steamers Benmore and Carrick Castle at the Broomielaw circa 1900

Clyde Steamers

From early Victorian times paddle steamers have carried commuters and tourists. At first there were small fleets and independent vessels, but by 1890 all ships were operated by the three main railway companies who had built railway lines to the Clyde coast piers such as Gourock and Wemyss Bay which respectively connected to steamer services to Dunoon and Rothesay.

By 1900 there were over 50 Clyde Steamers operating. There are still clues to the scale of this operation today. These include the wide walkway at Wemyss Bay station for the thousands of Rothesay-bound passengers, the signalling system at Kilcreggan to avoid conflicts at piers, and the large gents toilets at Rothesay pier needed to meet the needs of disembarking passengers.

Waverley was the only paddle steamer built after World War 2 for Clyde cruising. Motor vessels were more economical but after the war there was a shortage of fuel oil. In 1953 four motor vessels were built to replace the larger steamers. These were the Maids (of Argyll, Ashton, Cumbrae and Skelmorlie). The first purpose-built car ferries appeared in 1954. With increasing car-use and change in holiday habits the demand for Clyde cruising steadily declined. By 1964 there were eleven ships cruising the Clyde. These were the four Maids, three turbine steamers (TS), three paddle steamers (PS) and a diesel electric paddle vessel (DEPV), the Talisman.

TS Duchess of Montrose and PS Jeanie Deans were withdrawn at the end of the 1964 season followed by DEPV Talisman in 1966, PS Caledonia in 1969 and TS Duchess of Hamilton in 1970. Between 1970 and 1973, the Maids were taken out of service and one converted to a car ferry. Caledonian MacBrayne (CalMac) withdrew Waverley in 1973. Its remaining coastal steamer, TS Queen Mary, continued in service until 1977.

Photo: Iain Quinn
Saint Columba at Kyles of Bute - 1956

Photo: Iain Quinn
Duchess of Hamilton at Rothesay - 1948

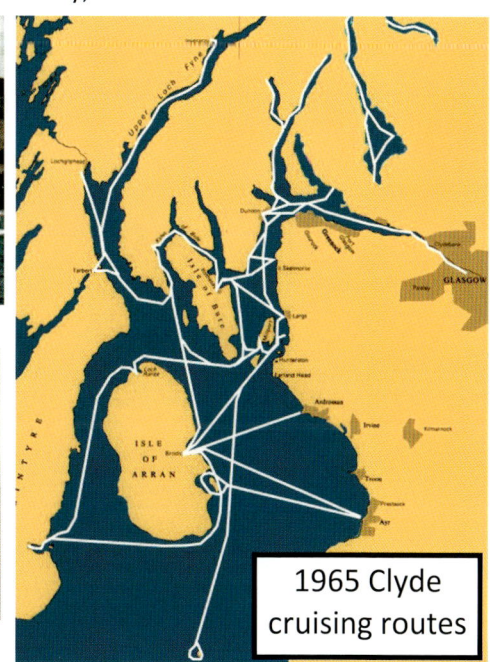

1965 Clyde cruising routes

A busy scene at Rothesay pier circa 1895. In foreground is PS Redgauntlet (1895, sold 1919)

Dunoon in 1939 with PS Juno (1937, sunk by bombs 1941) and, the world's first turbine-driven passenger ship, TS King Edward (1901 - 1952)

PS Jeanie Deans 1931 - 1964

Caledonia leaves Glasgow's Bridge Wharf in 1964

Waverley sails past Erskine Bridge under construction in 1970

- 14 -

The Firth's Towns

Bowling is the western end of the Forth & Clyde Canal which opened in 1790 and closed in 1963. The canal is 35 miles long. After 39 locks, it reaches Grangemouth on the Firth of Forth. In 2001, it was re-opened as part of the Millennium link project which connects it to Edinburgh via the Union Canal and Falkirk Wheel.

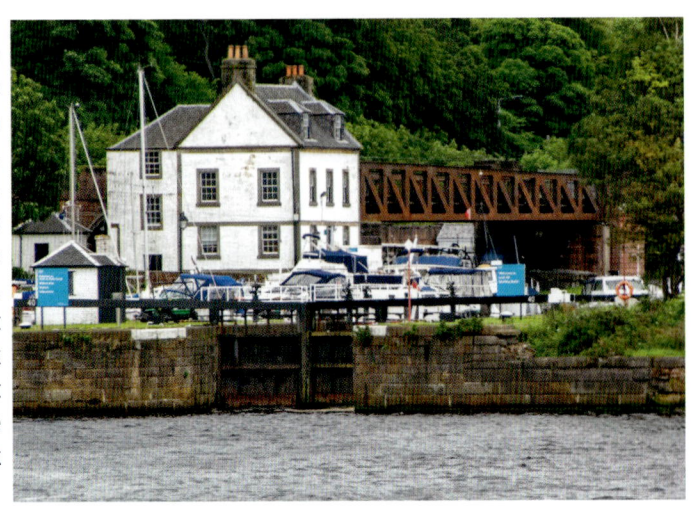

Dumbarton was first recorded as a settlement by Saint Patrick in the late 5th century. On the River Leven behind the castle was Denny's shipyard which closed in 1962. It had the world's first commercial ship testing tank which was built in 1883 and is now part of the Scottish Maritime Museum.

Port Glasgow was originally a small hamlet called Newark where a castle was built in 1478. In 1668 the Glasgow merchants purchased leased land to build a harbour that gave the town its name. At one time this was Glasgow's principal port but trade declined once sea-going ships could reach Glasgow. The first successful Paddle Steamer, the Comet, was built here in 1812. It was a prolific shipbuilding centre. Here, Scott–Lithgow built ships of 250,000 tons in two halves and joined them afloat in Greenock's Great Harbour.

Greenock had its original harbour built in 1710 as trade increased following the 1707 Act of Union. Scott's shipbuilding yard by the harbour was established in 1711. Sugar refineries, paper, cotton and woollen mills also contributed to the town's wealth. Its rail connection to Glasgow, opened in 1841, was the first for the Firth. The large and deep Great Harbour and James Watt Dock were built to compete with Glasgow. These opened in 1886. The clock tower at Custom House Quay was built by Rankin and Blackmore, who also built Waverley's engine.

Helensburgh was founded in 1776 and is laid out in the style of Edinburgh New Town. Henry Bell lived here and had the paddle steamer Comet built in 1812 to bring passengers from Glasgow. The inventor of television, John Logie Baird also was born here. Its railway to Glasgow opened in 1858.

Gourock became a popular seaside resort when its railway opened in 1889. This required a 1.2 mile rail tunnel, the longest in Scotland. The railway terminated at the pierhead to provide fast steamer connections to Dunoon and other piers.

Clock tower at Custom House Quay

Helensburgh's steep streets

- 16 -

Dunoon became an increasingly popular resort after direct steamers from Glasgow were introduced in the 1840s. The current pier was built in 1897. Above it the statue of Highland Mary who was one of Robbie Burns' lovers. The "Castle" was a large house built by the Lord Provost of Glasgow in 1824. It now houses a museum.

Wemyss Bay was a small settlement until 1865 when the railway and pier were opened. With increasing traffic a new station and pier were opened in 1903. This has an impressive glass canopy and a long wide walkway to the pier for the large numbers who transferred between trains and the Rothesay steamers.

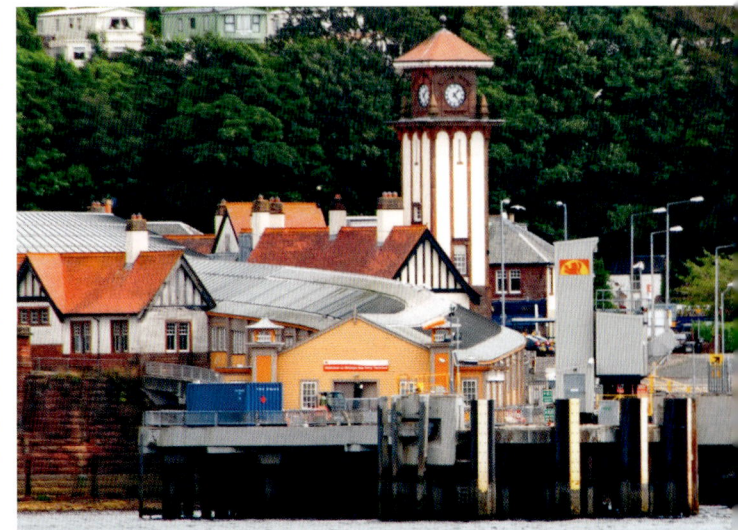

Largs became a popular holiday resort when its railway opened in 1895. The battle of Largs in 1263 was part of a failed Viking campaign against the Scots.

Rothesay castle dates back to the 13th century. The town became a very popular resort. In its heyday up to 100 steamers a day arrived here, hence the need for the large impressive gents toilet on the pier which opened in 1899. A tramway opened in 1882 to take holiday makers across the island to Ettrick Bay. Initially horse drawn, this was electrified in 1902 and closed in 1932. Its seafront Pavilion opened in 1938. During World War Two Rothesay was a submarine training base.

Ardrossan exported coal and iron in the early 17th century but needed a connection to Glasgow to expand. After an abortive canal scheme in 1806, the railway reached the port in 1840. Ferry services to Arran started in 1834, followed by a service to Belfast (1884 to 1976) and the Isle of Man (1892 to 1996). Between 1841 and 1848, the fastest route from London to Glasgow included a ship between Fleetwood and Ardrossan.

Irvine was given Burgh status in 1140. It was Glasgow's main harbour until the deepening of the Clyde in 18th century. Nobel Industries founded a factory for the manufacture of the explosive in 1870 on the isolated coast north of Irvine. To the south is the large Caledonian paper mill. Established in 1987, producing up to 280,000 tons of paper per year.

Prestwick developed in the 1840s as the arrival of the railway that enabled Glasgow's middle classes to move to large houses along the coast. It held the original Open Golf Championship in 1860 but was soon too small to accommodate the crowds so it was last held here in 1925. At 9,800 feet its airport has the longest runway in Scotland.

Ayr is an old town with a street plan established by 1200 when its river was first bridged. In 1315, Robert the Bruce held the first Scottish Parliament in Ayr. Until recent times Ayr flourished because of its harbour which, in the 14th century was Scotland's most important West Coast port. Robert Burns was born in nearby Alloway. It became a popular seaside resort with the opening of the railway in 1840.

1. The Clyde - from the city

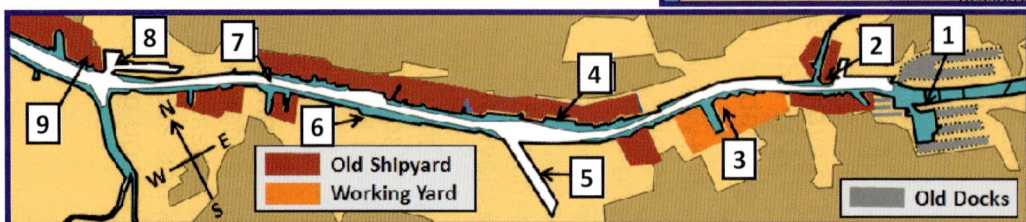

	Miles	Est Time	
1	0.0	0:00	**Pacific Quay** - Waverley's Glasgow berth was at the heart of a dock complex that had 4 miles of wharves. These have now been replaced by the BBC and SECC. To the north was Queen's Dock, opened 1877, on which the SECC stands today. To the west are three disused dry docks, the largest being 880 feet long.
2	0.6	0:05	**Riverside Museum** - was opened in 2011. Alongside is the Glenlee, built 1896 at Port Glasgow. It is on the site of A & J Inglis shipyard where Waverley was launched in 1946. Their yard closed in 1962.
3	1.1	0:08	**BAE Systems** - one of last Clyde shipbuilders. HMS Duncan's launch here in 2010 was probably the last on the Clyde. On the bank opposite are the new Meadowside Quay flats built on the site of four huge brick granaries that were demolished in 2007.
4	2.1	0:13	**Barclay Curle Crane** - One of six "Titan" cranes built on the Clyde of which four remain today. Around 60 such cranes were built worldwide. The adjacent building was the engine workshop whose roof opened to allow the crane to lift engines into ships.

Photo: Nick Wober

- 19 -

5	2.4	0.15	**King George V dock**—Opened in 1931 for larger ships and is the only operational dock within Glasgow city. It handles dry bulk cargoes, chemicals and industrial equipment.
6	3.0	0:18	**Braehead** - The shopping centre opened in 1999 on site of a former power station. In summer a river bus operates with eight stops between here and the city centre. Opposite is BAE Systems yard which was originally Yarrow Shipbuilders.
7	3.9	0:21	**Renfew Ferry** - Established in 1790, this is now the last of the many ferries across the river. Up to 1984 it was a car ferry. It was saved from closure in 2010 when Clydelink took over the service, replacing two 50 seat boats with one 12 seater.
8	4.9	0:25	**Rothesay Dock** - Built in 1907 for the coal trade it now handles gravel, sand and road salt and is used by aviation tankers. In 2005 the River Clyde Boatyard was established. It is the only one on the upper Clyde and has a 75 tonne boat lift.
9	5.1	0:26	**John Brown Shipyard** - Many famous ships built here including the Cunard Queens and HMS Hood. The slipways, which can be seen at low tide, point into the River Cart opposite so large ships could be launched. The 1907 **Titan Crane** lifted engines, boilers, gun turrets etc. to fit out ships. Restored in 2007, it is regularly open in summer offering great views and a Clyde shipbuilding exhibition.

The site of John Brown's yard is now the Clydebank campus of West College Scotland. All that remains is the Titan Crane and slipways which can be seen at low tide.

2. The Clyde - to the sea

"Glasgow made the Clyde, and the Clyde made Glasgow"

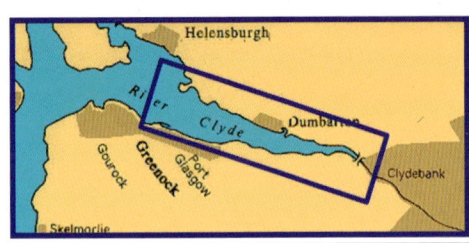

	Miles	Est Time	
10	6.2	0:30	**Golden Jubilee Hospital** - Built in 1994 on the site of one of the UK's largest shipyards, William Beardmore. Closed in 1930.
11	8.0	0:37	**Erskine Bridge** - Opened in 1971. The last of the Clyde's 61 bridges before the sea. In 1996 it was struck by an oil platform under tow. Repairs cost £4.3 million.
12	8.4	0:39	**Princess Louise Hospital** - Built in 1845, it became a hospital for limbless wounded of WW1. Today it is a 5 star hotel, whilst the Erskine Hospital behind it continues to care for forces veterans.
13	9.0	0:41	**Bowling** - The western end of the Forth & Clyde Canal which can take boats of 9.7 ft. headroom, 63ft long, 19.5 ft. wide, 6 ft. draft with 4 inches added to sea water draught to allow for fresh water buoyancy.
14	9.7	0:44	**Henry Bell Monument** - erected in 1838 commemorates Henry Bell (1767-1830) who pioneered Europe's first commercial steamship service on the Clyde using the 30 ton Comet paddle steamer which had a 3hp engine. This stands in front of the ruined **Dunglass** Castle, dating back to the mid 15th century.
15	10.0 - 12.0	0:45 - 0:53	The 2 mile **Lang Dyke** was built in 1773 to deepen the Clyde channel by increasing tidal scour.
16	11.2	0:50	**Dumbuck Crannog** - At low tide the piles of a 2000 year old wooden building can be seen in the mudflats on the northern bank. For those with GPS the map reference is NS415739.
17	12.2	0:54	**Dumbarton Castle** - is at the base of a 240 ft. high volcanic rock.

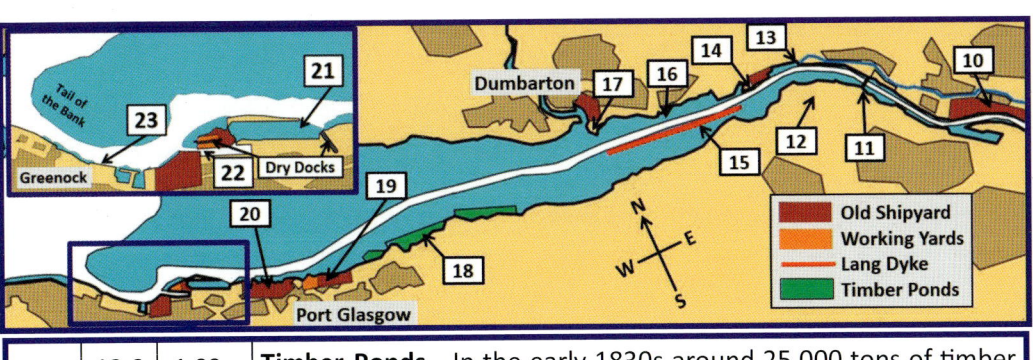

18	13.6 -15.5	1:00 - 1:07	**Timber Ponds** - In the early 1830s around 25,000 tons of timber per year was imported for shipbuilding. This was kept in ponds formed by upright timbers to be seasoned by salt water.
19	16.8	1:12	**Port Glasgow** - The seven storey brick building behind Newark castle was built as a sugar refinery and was taken over by the **Gourock Ropeworks** in 1886. Just west of the castle is **Ferguson Marine**, the last remaining shipbuilder on the lower Clyde who specialise in Roll-on/ Roll-off ferries.
20	17.3	1:14	**Tesco** - opened in 2007 on the site of Scott Lithgow shipyard. By the roundabout just east of Tesco is a replica of Henry Bell's Comet, built in 1962 for its 150th anniversary.
21	18.0	1:17	Just east of Greenock's **Great Harbour** is the 1000 ft. long Firth of Clyde dry dock. Today the dock is rarely used.
22	19.1	1:22	The **James Watt Dock** allowed Greenock to take larger ships using the Clyde. Its dry dock is 635 ft. long and is used by the Waverley. The **Titan crane** was built in 1917.
23	19.7	1:25	**Custom House Quay** is where Waverley berths at Greenock. Rankin and Blackmore, who built Waverley's engines, made the clock tower. The deep water channel by the quay opens out beyond Clydeport Ocean Terminal and the "Tail of the Bank", the name to the anchorage north of Greenock.

The River Clyde

Barclay Curle's Engine Workshop built in 1913. The Titan Crane was built in 1920.

The Renfrew ferry is the last of 11 ferries across the river. Seen here is the 'Yoker Swan', one of two ferries that were replaced by a single smaller pedestrian only ferry in 2010.

Waverley as seen from the Erskine Bridge

Photo: Murray Paterson

Waverley passing Scott Lithgow's yard at Port Glasgow in 1977 where the bow part of the 267,000 ton supertanker 'World Score' was being built. It was joined to the aft part in Greenock's Great Harbour. The site is now a Tesco store.

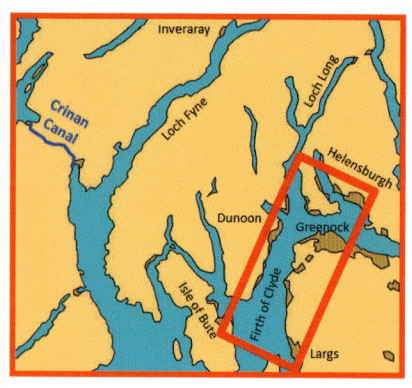

3. Firth of Clyde - North
The Channel

The Firth of Clyde Channel, a marked channel for deep draft vessels from Greenock to a point level with the southern tip of the Isle of Bute. In this area many crowded paddle steamers once carried holidaymakers and commuters to and from Glasgow.

1	**Helensburgh**—at the top of one of the town's steep streets is the Hill House built by Charles Rennie Mackintosh.
2	In 1974 the sugar ship Captayannis dragged its anchor in a storm and was holed when she then collided with a tanker. Being in imminent danger of sinking she was driven on a shallow sandbank and then capsized.
3	**Greenock's** wealth from its old trade and industries is evident from its 75 metres high Victoria Tower built in 1886. Its Clydeport terminal can accommodate cruise ships and other vessels too deep for the River Clyde channel.
4	**Gourock** From here there are passenger ferries to Dunoon and Kilcreggan. The outdoor swimming pool dates from when the town was a busy seaside resort.
5	Steamers brought **Kilcreggan** within easy reach of Glasgow wealthy who had grand houses there. Three circular windows on its pier were part of the Clyde Pier Signalling system required because of the large number of steamers.
6	The small village of **Blairmore** has had a pier since 1855 which ceased to be regularly used after 1973. Due to the work of the Friends of Blairmore Pier Trust, it was re-opened in 2005. The pier's heritage cabin depicts its history.
7	**Hunters Quay** is used by the Western Ferries and is the southern entrance to **Holy Loch**, so-called as a 6th century ship sank in the loch carrying soil from the Holy Land for Glasgow Cathedral. It was submarine base in WW2 and from 1961 to 1992 when it was an American Polaris base with a large floating dry dock.
8	**Dunoon** was a popular resort. Above the pier is the statue of Highland Mary, one of Robbie Burns' lovers. The "Castle" houses a museum.
9	**Cloch Point** lighthouse was built in 1797 as Clyde ports became important. In WW1 and WW2 an anti-submarine boom spanned the Firth from here to Dunoon.
10	Ferries leave **Wemyss Bay** for the Isle of Bute. The long wide walkway to the pier indicates the large numbers who caught the many steamers to Rothesay.
11	Markers denote the **Skelmorlie measured mile** of 6080 feet (a nautical mile). This dates from 1866 for full power trials of new and overhauled vessels.

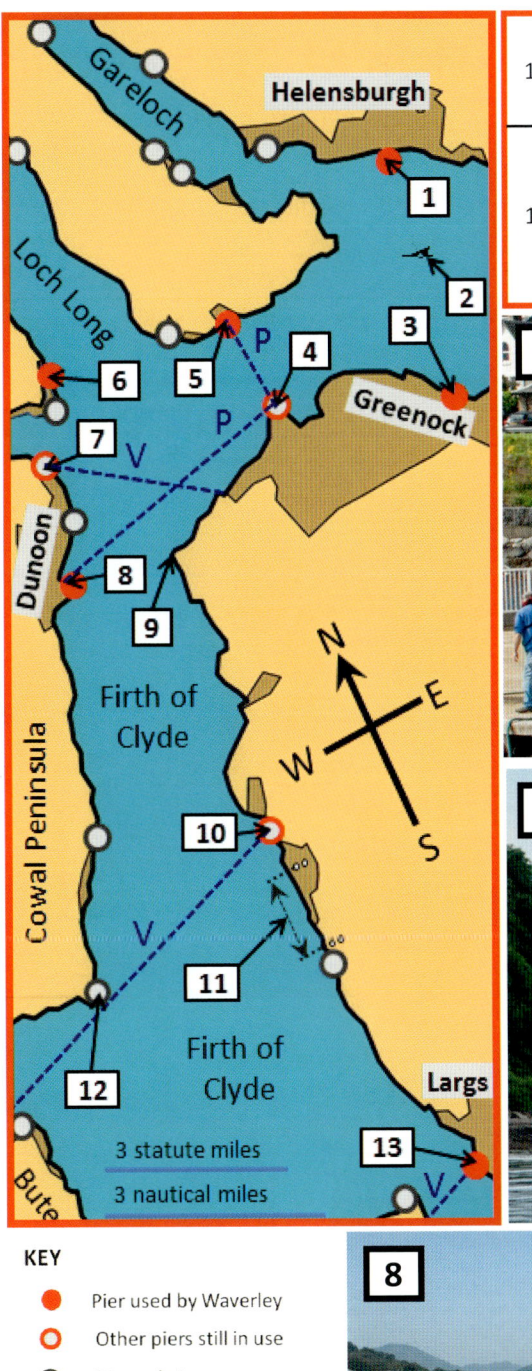

12	**Toward Point** - Cowal peninsula's southern tip. Its lighthouse was built in 1812.
13	**Largs** From here the CalMac vehicle ferry runs to Great Cumbrae island. The art deco building that can be seen from the pier is Nardini's Ice-Cream parlour.

KEY
- Pier used by Waverley
- Other piers still in use
- Disused pier
- ----- Ferry route (V)ehicular or (P)edestrian

- 26 -

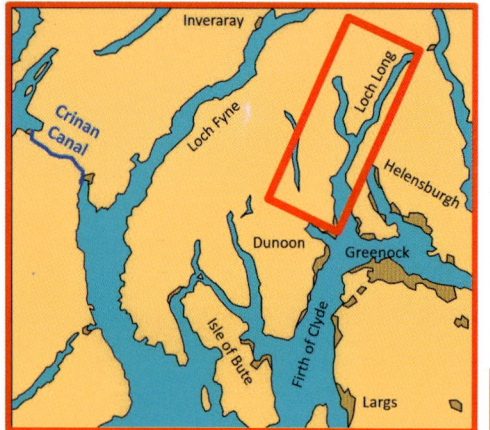

4. Firth of Clyde - North Loch Long

The indented coastline of the Kyles of Bute and Lochs Long, Goil and Fyne rival the Norwegian Fjords. For over 200 years paddle steamers have been the best way to see this wild and remote area, so close to Glasgow.

1	**Arrochar** is 1.7 miles from Loch Lomond and so was part of steamer tour on both lochs. At the loch's west side is the disused torpedo testing pier that fired test torpedoes. This opened in 1912 and fired its last torpedo in 1986.
2	**Lochgoilhead**, founded in 1750s is a village of 300–400.
3	**Finnart Oil terminal** has a pipeline to Grangemouth refinery and a deep water berth for tankers up to 324,000 tonnes. It was opened by the Clyde steamer Queen Mary II in 1959.
4	**Carrick Castle** is a 15th century tower house and was held by the Earls of Argyll. It was a ruin but was reroofed in the early 1990s.
5	**Coulport** holds the UK's stock of Trident nuclear warheads. Its two docks load Vanguard nuclear submarines. The covered berth is one of the world's largest floating concrete structures.
6	**Blairmore** has had a pier since 1855 for which regular use stopped after 1971. It was re-opened in 2005. The pier has a heritage cabin depicting its history.

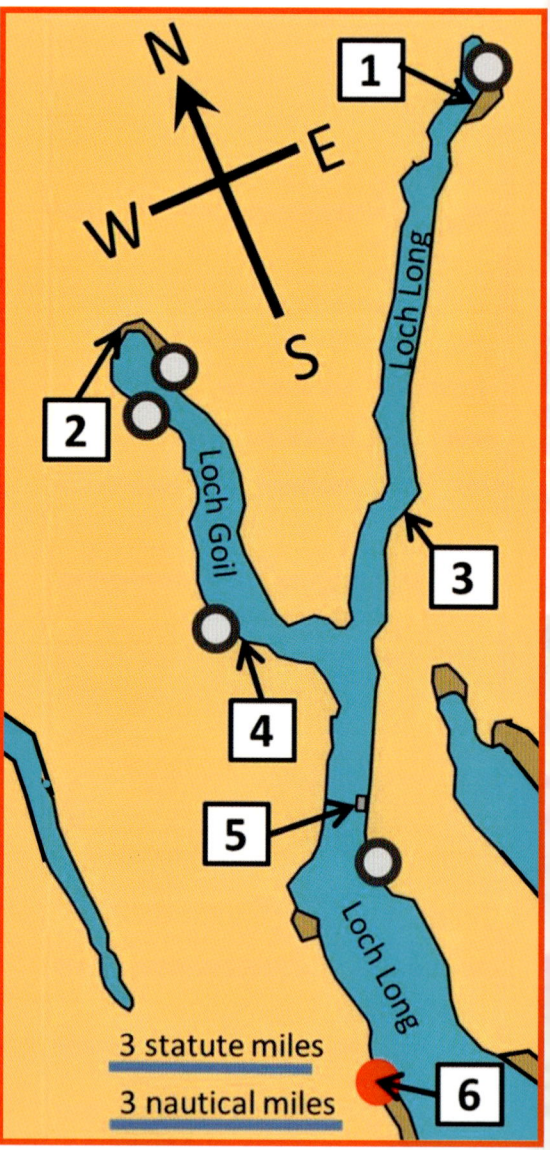

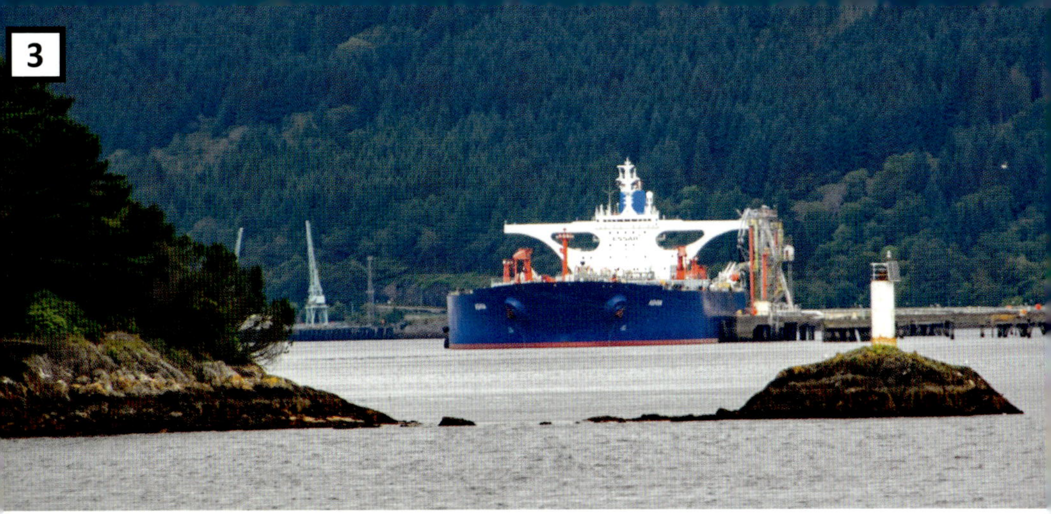
3

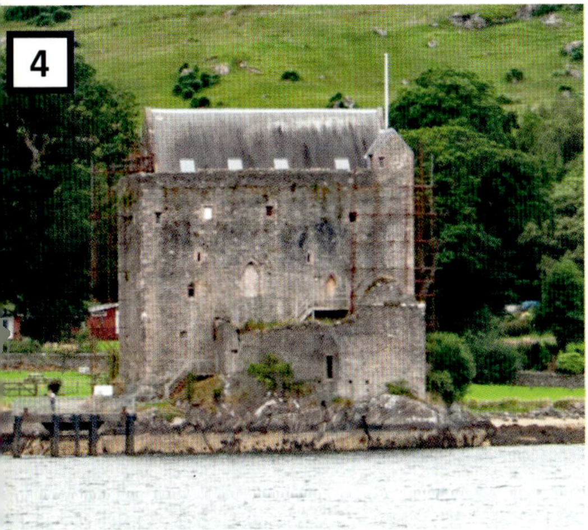
4

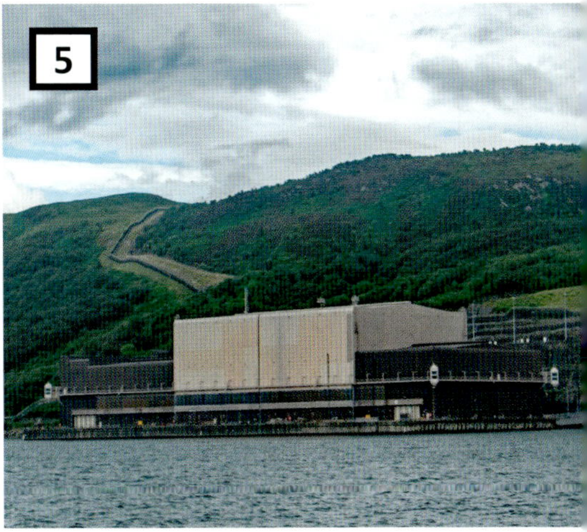
5

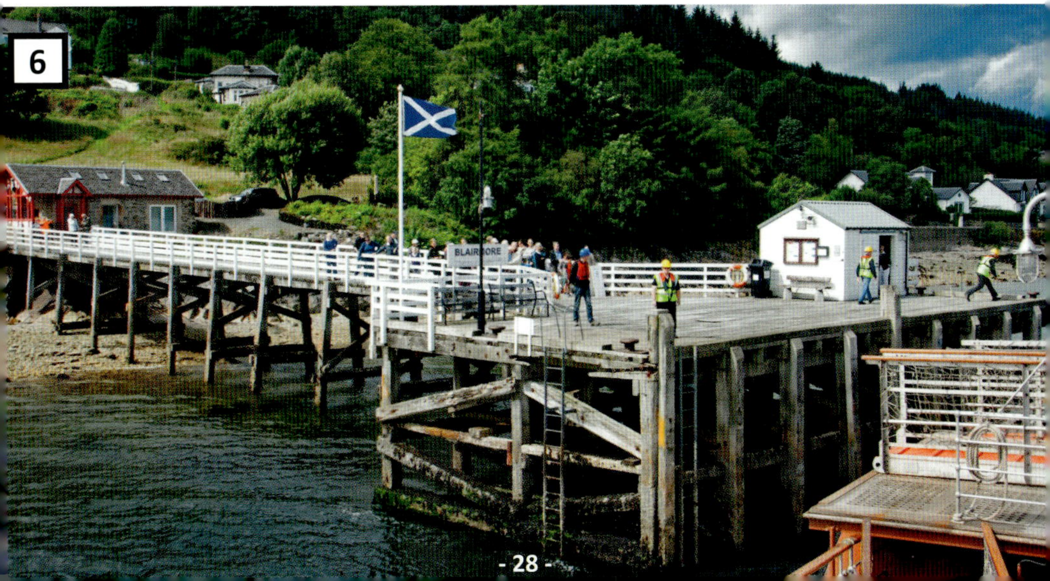

6

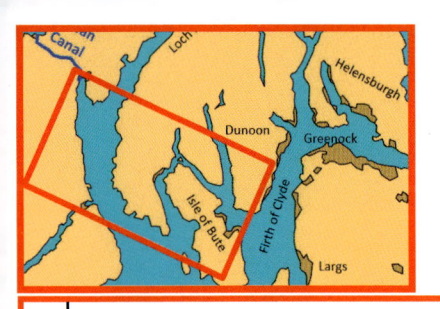

5. Firth of Clyde - North Rothesay and The Kyles of Bute

1	**Rothesay** has seafront gardens with a Winter Pavilion that has an exhibition about the town's steamers traffic. There is also an interesting museum and ruined castle. The impressive gents toilets on the pier can be visited by ladies on request.
2	In WW2 **Port Bannatyne** was a base for midget submarines (X craft) and human torpedo training. It has a memorial garden for those who served on these craft.
3	**Ardyne Point** was the site of an oil platform construction yard that built three concrete oil platforms between 1974 and 1978. At 300,000 tons, these were the largest floating objects ever built at the time.
4	**Loch Striven** is a sheltered deep sea loch sometimes used as a anchorage for laid up vessels. In WW2 it was used for X craft training and testing a smaller version of the bouncing bomb which was intended for use against battleships.
5	**Colintraive** in Gaelic means "swimming narrows" as cattle from Bute were swum across the strait on their way to market. The 400 yard narrows is now the "backdoor" ferry route to the Isle of Bute.
6	The **Kyles of Bute** main channel has two pairs of buoys between about 80 or 90 ft apart according to the state of the tide. With its 58 ft. beam Waverley's sail through the Kyles is spectacular and challenging. At high tide the ship may take the southerly dog leg channel next to the Isle of Bute.
7	**Tighnabruaich**'s pier was built in the 1830s. It is cared for by a pier association who have provided an exhibition in the former Pier Master's office. Until a new road was built in 1969 it depended on its sea route which allowed Glasgow businessmen to commute from here. The town has a sailing centre with its own school.
8	**Ardlamont Point** separates Loch Fyne and the Kyles of Bute. For some years a dolphin has regularly appeared as Waverley passes the buoy here.
9	**Tarbert** extends over the isthmus to West Loch Tarbert. In the past boats and goods were carried over the mile between the two lochs. It has a castle denoting its strategic location on the Kintyre peninsula.
10	The village of **Ardrishaig** is at the entrance to the Crinan Canal. It owes its existence to the canal which opened in 1801 to provide a route to the Western Isles that avoided the often hazardous sail around the Mull of Kintyre.
11	At 40 miles long, **Loch Fyne** is Scotland's longest sea loch. From Tarbert it is 30 miles to the loch's main town, Inveraray from where it is a further seven miles to the head of the loch. Loch Fyne is well-known for its oysters.

- 30 -

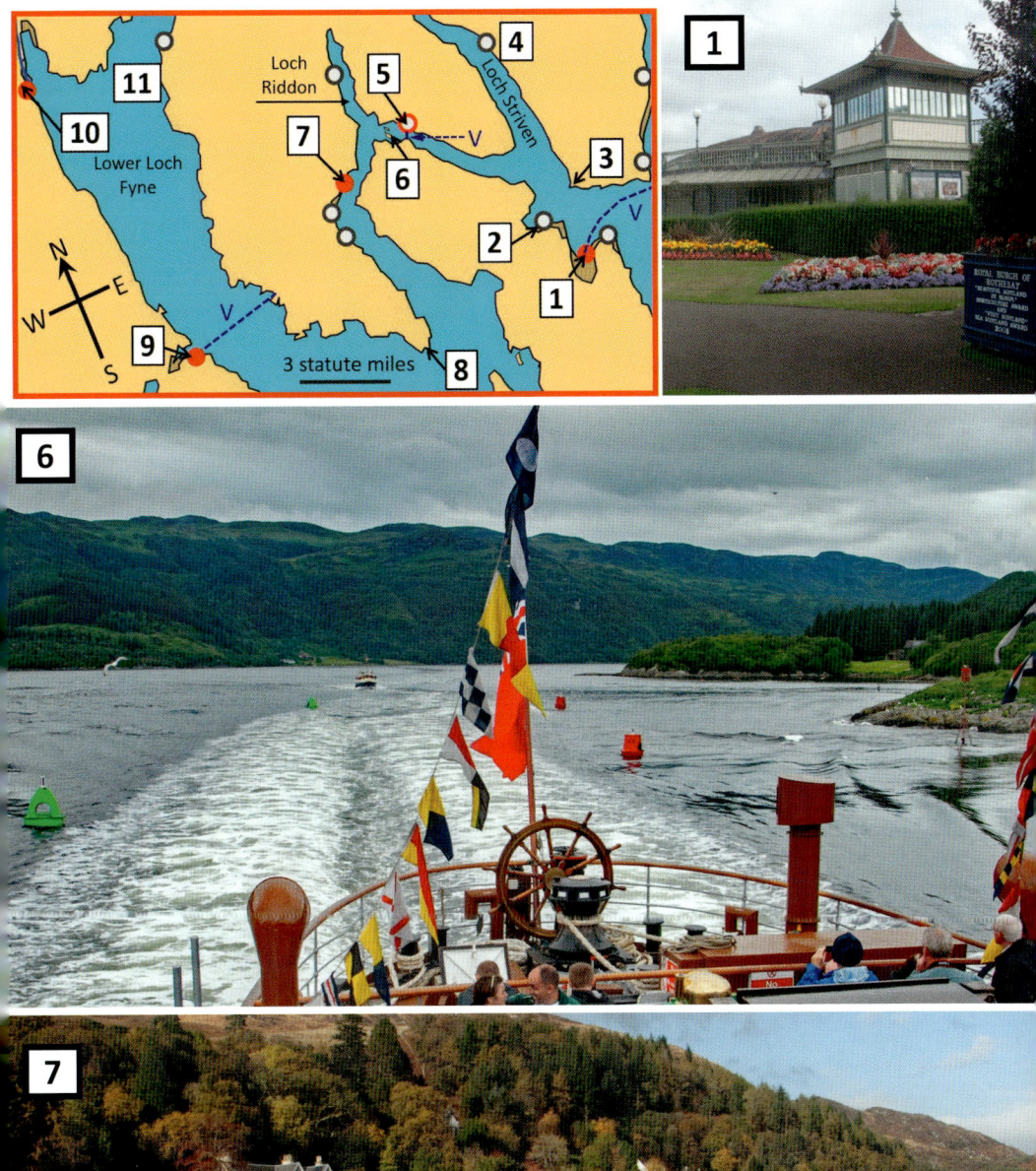

Firth of Clyde - North

Custom House and clock at Greenock

M.V. Loch Dunvegan at Rhubodach ready for its 400 yard crossing from Bute to Colintraive

M.V. Loch Riddon and Loch Shira on the busy crossing from Largs to Great Cumbrae

At Largs, Nardini's Art Deco Ice Cream parlour is the backdrop for waiting Waverley passengers.

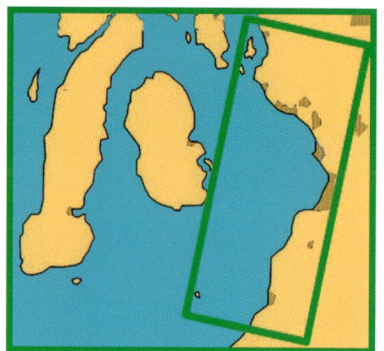

6. Firth of Clyde - South The Golf Coast

The Ayrshire coast has 20 or so golf courses. Its benign coastal weather keeps Prestwick Airport fog-free. Robert Burns was born just outside Ayr - "Auld **Ayr** wham ne'er a toun surpasses for honest men and bonnie lasses". Its ports of Irvine, Troon and Ayr have a rich maritime history.

1	From **Largs** the CalMac vehicle ferry runs to Great Cumbrae island. The art deco building that can be seen from the pier is Nardini's Ice-Cream parlour.
2	**Millport** on **Great Cumbrae Island** was a popular resort and has Britain's smallest cathedral. The island is 3.8 x 1.7 miles and is Scotland's most densely populated island. Waverley calls at Keppel pier, 1.5 miles from Millport, where there is the small Robertson museum and aquarium.
3	**Hunterston** has two of Scotland's four nuclear power stations. The 360 MW "A" station operated from 1964 to 1990. The still operational 1000 MW "B" station opened in 1976. The deep water terminal was originally for iron ore but now is used to import coal which is taken by rail to power stations, much to Yorkshire.
4	The Firth of Clyde's first navigation light was built on **Little Cumbrae** Island in 1757. It was an open fire lit at the top of a circular stone tower.
5	**Ardrossan** has had a ferry service to Arran since 1834 and car ferries since 1954. A summer service to Campbeltown was established in 2013.
6	**Irvine** has the **Scottish Maritime Museum** which has Waverley's original boiler on display. The large Caledonian paper mill is visible to the south of the town.
7	**Troon** golf course hosts the Open Golf Championship roughly every seven years.
8	**Lady Isle** has a perimeter of 1/2 miles and is only 20 ft. high. It is 2 miles SW of **Troon**. It has a ruined 15th century chapel and is a wild bird sanctuary. In 1776 there were a pair of beacons on the island to mark a nearby safe anchorage. In 1903 a lighthouse with external stairs was built on the site of one of the beacons.
9	**Prestwick** airport has the longest runway in Scotland (9,800 ft). Elvis Presley passed through the airport in 1960, the only time he set foot on British soil.
10	**Ayr** harbour is in the mouth of the River Ayr. It is now the only rail-connected harbour on the Clyde. With a population of 47,000, it is the largest town on the Firth. The Robert Burns museum is 3 miles to the south at Alloway, his birthplace.
11	The holiday camp at **Heads of Ayr** started life as a WW2 military camp. At the Admiralty's request, this was built by Billy Butlin who had opened two pre-war holiday camps. After the war it became Butlin's holiday camp. In 1999 it became Craig Tara Caravan Holiday Park managed by Haven Holidays.

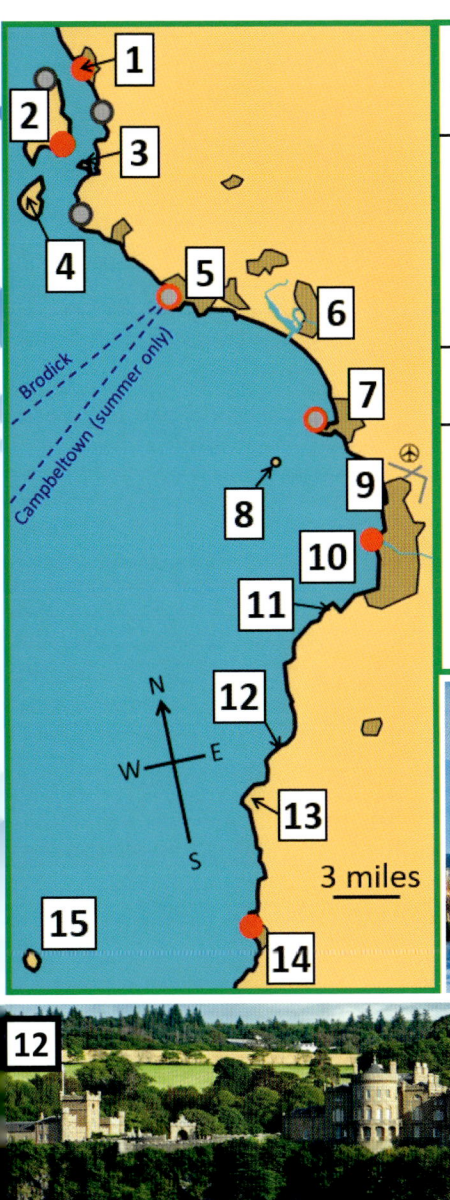

12	**Culzean Castle** dates from 1777. It is owned by National Trust for Scotland and is one of their most popular visitor attractions.
13	There is another Open Championship golf course at **Turnberry.** In both world wars some of it was flattened for a training airfield. There is a prominent memorial to the estimated 200 who died training. The lighthouse was built in 1873.
14	**Girvan** was originally a fishing port and has a population of around 8,000
15	2 miles in circumference and 1109ft high, **Ailsa Craig** is 10 miles West of Girvan and known as Paddy's milestone as it was on the Glasgow to Belfast ferry route. Huge numbers of gannets nest in its bird sanctuary. Its granite has unique qualities making it ideal material for curling stones.

- 34 -

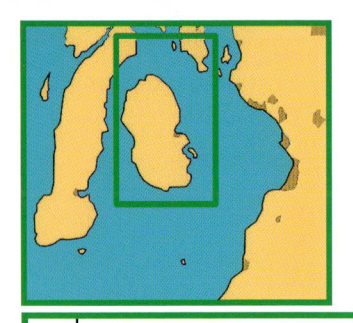

7. Firth of Clyde - South Arran and South Bute

Arran is described as Scotland in miniature

1	**Mount Stuart** on Bute is considered to be the finest domestic architecture from Britain's Gothic revival in the 19th century. It also has extensive gardens.
2	**Skipness** has a ruined 13th century castle. Its Kilbrannan Chapel also dates from this time and has some rare carved medieval tombstones.
3	**Lochranza** has a 16th century castle and, since 1995, a distillery. Its ferry runs to Claonaig. Across Loch Ranza from the pier is Newton Point. Here in 1787, James Hutton "father of modern geology" first found evidence that showed the earth was much older than previously thought.
4	The **Arran Measured Mile** is actually two measured (nautical) miles of 1854 and 1851 metres on a course of 142° or 322°. It was built by the Admiralty, as big ships using the Skelmorlie measured mile needed more sea room and their wash caused problems. It was first used by HMS Renown in 1916. RMS Queen Mary did her sea trials here in March 1936 as did QE2 in 1969.
5	**Brodick** is the island's main commercial centre and ferry port and has the Isle of Arran Heritage museum. Its red sandstone baronial castle and gardens are open to the public.
6	**Lamlash** - Arran's largest village with its only secondary school and hospital. The bay is a natural anchorage protected by Holy Island. It is Scotland's first No Take Zone with all fishing banned.
7	**Holy Island** - 2 miles long, 0.6 miles wide and 1110 ft. high and home to Buddhist Peace Centre.
8	**Whiting Bay** had the longest pier on the Clyde. It operated from 1899 to 1962 and was demolished in 1964.

9	The teardrop-shaped **Island of Pladda** is less than a mile long. It has an early lighthouse built in 1790 before lighthouses had identifying flashes. For this reason there are separate upper and lower lighthouses to identify its location.
10	Just north of **Blackwaterfoot** is an Iron Age hill fort at Drumadoon Point. Just north of this is King's Cave where in 1306-7, a spider is said to have inspired King Robert the Bruce.

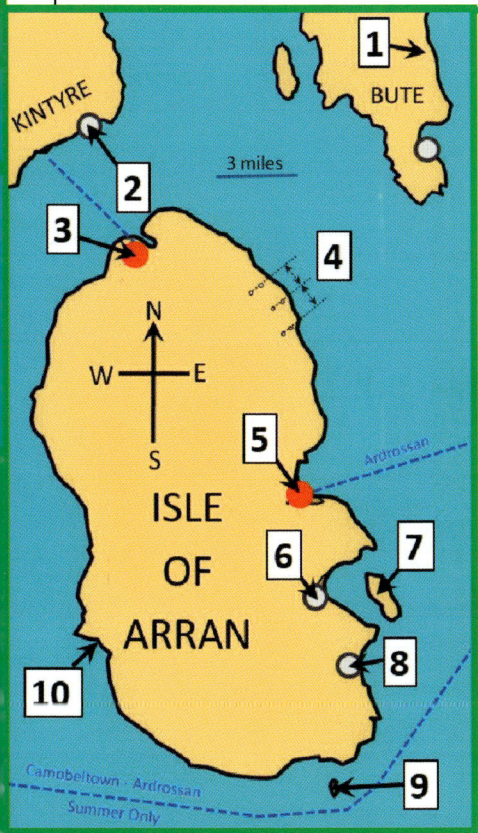

Arran is the seventh largest Scottish Island with an area of 169 square miles and a 56 mile long coast road which circumnavigates the island. It is a mountainous island with the highest point being Goat Fell at 2,866 ft and is popular with geologists who come to see its complex varying features.

Arran has been continuously populated for thousands of years so has many pre-historic remains. In 2011 its population was 4,629.

Waverley approaches Arran

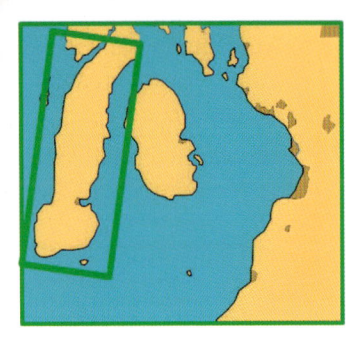

8. Firth of Clyde - South Kintyre

The Kintyre peninsula is 30 miles long by 11 miles wide. With few roads across it, its interior is one of the most remote places in Britain.

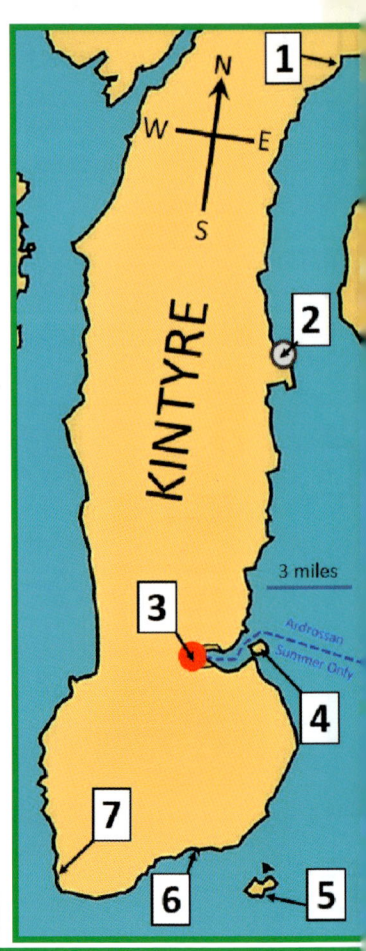

1	**Skipness** has a ruined 13th century castle. Its Kilbrannan Chapel also dates from this time and has some rare carved medieval tombstones.
2	**Carradale** had a thriving herring industry. Its pier was built in 1858 to give a daily steamer service to Glasgow up to World War Two.
3	**Campbeltown** has 3 distilleries and is one of 5 Scottish whisky regions. Its museum and heritage centre is worth a visit.
4	**Davaar Island** and its lighthouse is at the head of Campbeltown loch. It can be reached on foot at low tide.
5	The lighthouse on **Sanda Island** was built in 1850.
6	**Southend** has an 18 hole golf course. Here Saint Columba is said to have first set foot in Scotland. East of its bay is Dunaverty Point on which there was a castle.
7	The **Mull of Kintyre** is 12 miles from Ireland. Its lighthouse built in 1788 was one of Scotland's first. It is also the title of a 1991 song by Paul McCartney which, at 2.1 million copies, remains the UK's best-selling non-charity single.

Low flying gannets round the Mull of Kintyre.

Firth of Clyde - South

Waverley arriving at Ayr.

Unusual design of lighthouse and bird observatory on the 650 yard long Lady Isle near Troon.

Gannets on Ailsa Craig

Girvan departure

Waverley is owned by Waverley Steam Navigation Company (WSN) whose major shareholder is the PSPS. She is operated by Waverley Excursions Limited (WEL). WSN is a charity registered in Scotland, number SC005832. WEL is a non-profit making organisation. Both companies have offices at 36, Lancefield Quay, Glasgow G3 8HA.

All fares and donations from public and local authorities help keep Waverley sailing.

Waverley sails on the Clyde in June, July and August. She also sails in the following areas:

- Scottish Western Isles
- Liverpool and Llandudno
- Bristol Channel
- English South Coast
- London and Thames

Photo: Roy Tait

To view timetables and book tickets visit **www.waverleyexcursions.co.uk** or call 0845 130 4647.
Sailing tickets are also available from VisitScotland information centres or can usually be purchased on board when you sail.

The hills of the Cowal peninsula form the backdrop as Waverley is seen off Kilcreggan

Waverley at Helensburgh

Waverley under CalMac ownership in 1973

Photo: PSPS Collection

The PSPS Scottish Branch would like to acknowledge the work of David Shirres who produced this guide, supplied its graphics and, unless otherwise acknowledged, the photographs. Particular thanks are also due to Iain Quinn and Gordon Wilson for their support and advice.

The Paddle Steamer Preservation Society (PSPS)

PSPS is proud to have saved two paddle steamers for the nation. The Society purchased PS Kingswear Castle in 1967 for the sum of £600 and was gifted PS Waverley in 1974 for just £1.

The Scottish Branch of the PSPS was formed in 1969 and has a current membership of around 800. It regularly organises charters and outings including an annual evening fundraising cruise on Waverley in addition to a Festive Cruise in association with the Coastal Cruising Association.

Branch members assist in the winter refit and maintenance of PS Waverley and also raise funds on board for her continued operation. In recent years the Branch has returned handsome donations to help maintain Waverley in operation.

For more information, up to date news about PSPS and to join the Society visit **www.paddlesteamers.org**

All proceeds from this guide help Waverley to continue sailing.

Paddle Steamer Preservation Society
A Company Limited by Guarantee
No 2167853 (England & Wales)
A Charity Registered in
England & Wales (298328)
and in Scotland (SC037603)
Registered Office: 17 Stock Field Close,
Hazlemere, High Wycombe, HP15 7LA

ISBN 9780993590108

v2.0 30.04.2016

Enjoyed your cruise? - Try another part of the Clyde

View timetables and book your next cruise at
www.waverleyexcursions.co.uk or by phoning 0845 130 4647.